A History of Fashion and Costume
Volume 8
The Twentieth Century

Clare and Adam Hibbert

☑® Facts On File, Inc.

The Twentieth Century

Copyright © 2005 Bailey Publishing
Associates Ltd

Produced for Facts On File by
Bailey Publishing Associates Ltd
11a Woodlands
Hove BN3 6TJ

Project Manager: Roberta Bailey
Editor: Alex Woolf
Text Designer: Simon Borrough
Artwork: Dave Burroughs, Peter Dennis,
    Tony Morris
Picture Research: Glass Onion Pictures
Consultant: Tara Maginnis, Ph.D.
Associate Professor of the University of Alaska,
Fairbanks, and creator of the website, The
Costumer's Manifesto (http://costumes.org/).

Printed and bound in Hong Kong

Facts On File, Inc.
132 West 31st Street
New York NY 10001

Facts On File books are available at special
discounts when purchased in bulk quantities for
businesses, associations, institutions, or sales
promotions. Please call our Special Sales
Department in New York at 212/967-8800 or
800/322-8755.

You can find Facts On File on the World Wide Web
at: http://www.factsonfile.com

Library of Congress Cataloging-in-Publication Data

Hibbert, Clare, 1970–
A history of fashion and costume.
   Volume 8, The Twentieth
Century/Clare and Adam Hibbert.
      p. cm.
Includes bibliographical references and
   index.
   ISBN 0-8160-5951-9
   1. Clothing and dress—History—
20th century.
   GT596.H53 2005
   391/.009/04—dc 22   2005046936

The publishers would like to thank the
following for permission to use their
pictures:

Art Archive: 6, 16, 24, 39 (bottom)
Corbis: 58
Kobal: 20, 23, 26, 30 (right), 39 (top),
43, 45
Mary Evans Picture Library: 9 (both),
17, 29,
Popperfoto: 12, 21,
Rex Features: 7 (top), 30 (left), 32, 37
(both), 41 (both), 42, 46, 47 (left), 48
(right)
Topham: 7 (bottom), 8, 18, 19, 27, 28,
33, 35, 36, 44, 47 (right), 48 (left), 49,
50, 53 (both), 54, 56, 57, 59
Victoria & Albert Museum: 10, 11, 14,
15, 55

Contents

Introduction

This volume traces the history of fashion and costume during the twentieth century, a period that saw the most rapid and revolutionary changes in dress so far.

Home-sewn clothing declined as mass-production techniques were introduced and people were able to buy cheap, factory-made clothes. Over the century, fashions for men, women, and children became far less restrictive. This partly reflected changes in society, as rules about "polite" behavior relaxed. People's roles changed, too. Women campaigned for and won the right to vote and play a more active role in society. Dress styles worn during previous centuries, when a wealthy woman's role was mostly decorative, were no longer appropriate.

New synthetic materials meant that clothes could perform better in extreme or even hazardous environments. Clothes also became easier to care for. Some new materials were developed during the century's many conflicts and wars; others were side effects of technological advances, such as space travel.

The biggest development of the twentieth century was the amazing improvement in global communications. Within decades of the first powered flight, air travel became relatively cheap. More people were able to travel abroad, encountering different forms of dress for the first time. Most importantly, the period saw the birth and development of cinema, television, and finally the Internet. These new media helped to spread all forms of culture, including fashion, straight into people's homes. American films and popular culture became dominant, and American jeans were soon a favorite garment all over the world. At the same time as this globalization of fashion, national costumes and traditional dress declined.

Chapter 1: The Noughties

The dawn of the twentieth century was a time of excitement and optimism. The first skyscrapers were appearing on the skylines of cities such as Chicago and New York. In Paris, France, the World's Fair of 1900 gave countries from around the world the chance to show off their latest achievements and inventions. Powered flight was just around the corner — the Wright brothers mastered it in December 1903.

The new century promised many changes and improvements, but at first, fashion remained much the same as it had been at the end of the nineteenth century. Styles for men, women, and children were extremely restrictive.

Underneath their walking dresses, restrictive corsets molded women's bodies, throwing the bust forward and the hips back to create a curvy S-bend shape.

Hourglass Figures

For fashionable women at the turn of the century, the ideal body had an ample bosom, tiny waist, and large hips. Known as the hourglass or S-bend (because it followed the curves of a letter "S"), this silhouette was achieved by wearing a rigid, boned corset. Helped by their maids, fashionable women usually changed clothes several times a day, wearing different outfits for morning, afternoon, and evening.

Daytime clothes covered the whole body. Whether in dresses or separates, women wore high collars, puffed-out bodices, and full skirts, worn over layers of rustling petticoats. Clothes were generally made by hand and involved enormous amounts of labor. Some dresses were embroidered with tiny flowers or draped with lace. Bodices or blouses were often

Mariano Fortuny (1871–1949)

The Spanish-born designer Fortuny spent time studying painting, drawing, chemistry, and dyes before turning to fashion design. During the 1890s, while building theatrical stage sets, he started to think more about the effects of light. Fortuny developed a special way of pleating silk, which created interesting plays of light. One of his earliest dresses was the Delphos gown (1906), a simple tunic made of pleated silk satin, inspired by the costume of classical Greece.

Three gowns by Mariano Fortuny.

pintucked, or decorated with sewn-on ribbons and bows.

From Teatime to Evening

The one time of day when women could escape their tight corsets was late afternoon. The tea gown was a loose, flowing gown worn before dressing for dinner. Comfortable but elegant, it was often made of light, floaty fabrics such as crêpe de chine, chiffon, or tulle. The most glamorous tea gowns were designed by exclusive couturiers, such as Lucile, Jacques Doucet, and Fortuny.

In the evening, wealthy women's dresses still swept the floor—some even had trains—but necklines plunged to reveal daring amounts of bosom. Sparkling beads and sequins decorated dresses, purses, and shoes.

Hats and Hairstyles

Long necks were considered very beautiful, so women wore their long hair up to emphasize the neck. Hats were usually covered with ostentatious feathers from ostriches, osprey, and birds of paradise—or were even decorated with whole stuffed birds.

Caring for Clothes

Middle- and upper-class families employed servants who kept their houses and their clothes clean. Some families used washerwomen or even commercial laundries. Cleaning clothes was a labor-intensive business. Clothes were supported on a wooden washboard and scrubbed clean using a brush, water, and soap. Manual washing machines, which had been invented in the United States in the 1840s, rubbed clothes between two curved surfaces. The first electric clothes washers appeared around 1900. They had a motor-driven spinning tub, but were not very reliable. They often caused electric shocks or shredded delicate clothes.

Manual washers were manufactured until the 1920s. Turning the lever moved one of the curved surfaces inside the tub over the other, rubbing the wet clothes in between.

At Work and Play

This young golfer epitomizes the fashionable "Gibson Girl" look. Tall, poised, and self-assured, she wears a shirt and jacket with a long, flowing skirt.

Women at Work

The satins, silks, and tulles worn by ladies of leisure were impractical for the growing numbers of independent middle-class women who went out to work. Sensible suits, known as tailor-mades, were aimed at governesses, typists, and store assistants. Made of hard-wearing tweed, which did not show the dirt, tailor-mades were also worn by wealthier women for traveling. They were teamed with a blouse which could be changed and washed more often.

Wearing separates, rather than an all-in-one dress, was popularized in the United States by an illustrated character known as the Gibson Girl. Created by artist Charles Gibson, she represented the new, modern woman and was often shown taking part in activities such as bicycling or playing tennis.

Men's Dress

Businessmen wore black morning coats with pinstriped trousers. Tweed or checked three-piece suits—a matching jacket, vest, and trousers—were also worn. All respectable men wore a hat outdoors, such as a derby, trilby, or even a straw boater.

On formal occasions, men still dressed in a top hat and frock coat, as they had in the 1800s. Originally based on a military coat, the frock coat was knee-length, came in at the waist, and was full at the back with pleats, buttons, and vents. It was worn with a vest and checked or pinstriped trousers.

Motoring Outfits

By the turn of the century, cars had been around for about twenty years, but were so expensive that only the very rich could afford them. From 1908, however, car ownership rose, with the introduction of the first mass-produced car, the Model T Ford.

The growing craze for motoring demanded specialist costumes. Early cars were open-topped and many lacked even a windscreen—motorists were soon covered with dirt thrown up from the roads. In summer, people wore duster coats, silk or linen overcoats that repelled the dust. Goggles, veiled bonnets, or balaclava-style helmets protected the eyes. In winter, travelers had to cope with mud, wet, and cold. They wore heavy overcoats of tweed, leather, or fur and usually snuggled up under a thick, woolen traveling blanket.

Bicycling Outfits

The bicycle was far more affordable, and popular with the lower and middle classes. Like the car, this relatively new form of transport required some adaptations to dress. Skirts were impractical, so separated skirts, known as bloomers, were worn instead. Bloomers were named after Amelia Bloomer, a nineteenth-century American who campaigned for reforms in women's dress.

Children's Craze

While most children's clothes were smaller versions of adult fashions,

Above: King Edward VII of England, Tsar Nicholas II of Russia, and the young princes. English naval uniforms—from blazers to sailor suits—were a major influence on men's dress.

Left: A drive in the country. People wore protective goggles and beekeeper hats to keep the dust out of their eyes, nose, and mouth.

there was one exception: the sailor suit. It first became popular in the 1840s, when Britain's Queen Victoria dressed her oldest son, then four, in an outfit based on traditional English naval dress. The sailor suit was still standard dress for young boys in the noughties.

Sweatshops

Invented around 1830, the sewing machine was used to make most clothes by the early twentieth century. Seamstresses usually worked extremely long hours for very low wages. Much of this "sweated labor" consisted of poor women who took in piles of sewing and worked from home. Other women—and children—worked together in factories known as sweatshops for their poor conditions. "Sweated labor" was most common in cities with a high population of poor, desperate immigrants. New York City, for example, became a center of the garment-making trade. From the 1910s, the trade union movement worked to end sweated labor in the Western world, but the problem continued, as manufacturing moved to poorer parts of the globe.

Chapter 2: The Teens

In the early 1910s, many women began to wear empire-line dresses, which had a low-cut neckline and exaggeratedly high waist.

The period from 1910 to 1919 was dominated by World War I, known at the time as the Great War (1914–1918). Just as people were coming to terms with the staggering loss of lives in the trenches, a worldwide influenza epidemic claimed millions more lives.

People began to question the old social order. In Russia, the royal family was overthrown in the revolutions of 1917. The revolutionaries tried to free women from unpaid housework, cooking, and laundry. Equality for women was also a big issue across Europe and America, although women only began to achieve full voting rights the following decade, for example in the United States (1920), Sweden (1921), and Britain (1928). Clothing reflected women's changing status, becoming generally less restrictive and more practical.

Reshaping the Body

For women, a new, straighter silhouette became fashionable, with less emphasis on the breasts and hips. There was even a revival of the high-waisted empire-line dress, originally made popular by the French empress Josephine in the early 1800s.

Corsets were no longer so tight and waist-pinching and were worn with long drawers. Women also wore a bust bodice to support the bosom. The brassière was patented in 1914 by the American Mary Phelps Jacobs. She is said to have constructed her first bra from two handkerchiefs and a length of ribbon.

This 1910 painting of a "Sack-Race" for wearers of "hobble" skirts pokes gentle fun at the fashion of the moment as a substitute for the sack.

The Hobble Skirt

Although the general trend was toward greater comfort, there was a notable exception. In 1911, French designer Paul Poiret created a long, narrow skirt that tapered in at the ankle. It allowed little room for movement, and the wearer could take only tiny steps. Before long, the style had a nickname: the "hobble skirt." Despite its impracticality, it remained fashionable until just before the war.

Oriental Influences

Eastern-style clothes were popular with wealthy women early in the decade, then revived after the war.

Kimonos, silk pajamas, baggy harem pants, tunic dresses, and turbans were made in colorful silks and brocades. Fabrics featured bold, exotic prints and were trimmed with tassels, feathers, or fur. This was another look championed by Paul Poiret but, unlike the hobble skirt, it was very comfortable and wearable.

Poiret was one of the decade's most important designers. He produced illustrated brochures that showed off his designs, and in 1912 and 1913 he toured major cities across Europe and the United States with a group of models, putting on catwalk shows.

An original costume worn in the *Ballets Russes* 1910 production of *Schéhèrazade*. It was designed by Leon Bakst.

Ballet Costumes

The popularity of exotic, eastern styles was partly inspired by the costumes worn by the famous Russian ballet, or Ballets Russes. Between 1909 and 1910, the company wowed audiences in Paris with their productions of Cléopâtre and Schéhèrazade, set in the exotic locations of Egypt and Persia. The dancers' flamboyant costumes were designed by Russian artist Léon Bakst. The bright colors and rich patterns captured people's imaginations after the previous decade's preference for muted, pastel shades.

Harsh Conditions

Extreme Clothing

Just as World War I broke out, English explorer Ernest Shackleton set off for Antarctica aboard Endurance. Thick fur gloves and boots protected his hands and feet from frostbite.

Leather and rubber are naturally water resistant, but cumbersome when wet. Waterproof gabardine, invented by Thomas Burberry around 1880, would become the preferred choice for explorers. Mountain climbers wore a gabardine suit over layers of woolen underwear, flannel shirts, and sweaters. Gabardine gloves covered woolen mittens underneath. To protect his face, one climber attempting Everest wore a fur-lined leather motorcycling helmet, with glass goggles and a leather mask.

Polar explorers also favored gabardine over-garments, but their gloves and boots were sewn from thick fur, such as seal or bearskin. Most wore balaclavas of leather or wool. However, right at the end of the previous decade, the American Robert Peary set out for the North Pole in an Inuit-style, all-in-one fur suit.

Women at War

During the war, women adopted more sober, military styles. Many helped the war effort by taking over jobs in factories and farms. Shorter, fuller skirt styles allowed greater movement, and some women even adopted trousers in the form of jodphurs or boilersuits. Almost as shockingly, they cut their hair into short styles that were easier to care for and less likely to get caught up in machinery.

Fighting Fashions

New technologies used in the war,

Lifting the Spirits

Despite its frivolity, fashion played an important part in the war, helping to keep up people's spirits. Styles for women in particular became extremely practical, but there was one outlet for fantasy. *Vogue* magazine had begun in the United States in 1892, but was launched in Britain in 1916. The magazine provided some sort of escapism from the wartime horrors and suffering.

such as aircraft and tanks, affected the uniforms worn. Aircraft had been used in the Italian-Turkish war of 1911, but their military use was really exploited for the first time during World War I. Initially, planes were used for reconnaissance, discovering the whereabouts of enemy lines. Later, bombers were introduced to hit enemy targets from the air.

Early warplanes had open cockpits. Typically a pilot wore a short leather coat with thigh-high leather boots. The hands and face were protected with gauntlets, a face mask, and balaclava, all made of leather. Pilots' goggles were made from anti-splinter glass. Many items of pilots' dress were lined with sheepskin or fur for extra warmth. Some Canadian pilots wore coats with ocelot-fur collars.

The war on the Western Front was fought from defensive trenches, which soon filled with rainwater and mud. For those who had boots, waterproofing them was a daily job. Long coats helped to keep off the rain. Trenchcoats were military-style gabardine overcoats with epaulets, wide lapels, and a belt at the waist. Simpler in style, the greatcoat was made of heavy wool, which gave more warmth in winter, but stayed wet longer.

Armor was introduced to protect against enemy artillery fire. A steel helmet protected the head. From 1916, German machine-gunners were also issued with body armor that covered the chest and stomach. The lower part was made up of articulated plates, to allow some movement.

Color and Camouflage

In the days when straightforward battles were fought above ground, it had been essential to easily identify the enemy and one's own side. As warfare changed, so did uniforms. British troops began to dress in khaki during the Boer War (1899–1902), but at the outbreak of World War I, some French soldiers still dressed in red woolen trousers and blue coats. By the end of the war, troops on all sides made use of khaki, field gray, and camouflage to avoid becoming a target of long-range enemy fire.

It was cold and wet in the trenches. Soldiers wrapped woolen puttees around their shins for extra warmth and wore gabardine trenchcoats to keep off the rain.

Chapter 3: The Twenties

K nown as the Roaring Twenties, the decade that followed the war was a time of excess and partying–for the rich at least. Relieved to be alive, the young indulged in the latest dance crazes, listened to jazz on the radio, and went to the movies. *The Jazz Singer* (1927) was the first "talkie," or film with sound. Before then, people watched silent movies with musical accompaniment.

A low-waisted, flapper-style evening gown from the Paris-based fashion house, Worth. It is accessorized with an exotic fan, while bangles and bracelets emphasize the bare arms.

The twenties saw greater freedom for women, as suffragettes' protests finally paid off and many gained the vote for the first time. Married women also had the option of planning their families: Margaret Sanger had opened her first birth control clinic in the United States in 1916, and Marie Stopes opened Britain's first in 1921.

Not everyone enjoyed the twenties. Some of the young men who had survived the war suffered a mental disorder known as shell shock, haunted by the horrors they had witnessed. And the twenties ended with the devastating stockmarket crash of 1929, which marked the beginning of a decade of economic depression.

Flappers!

"Flapper" was the name given to fun-loving young women in the twenties. Flappers wore shockingly short skirts—some just below the knee—and hid any womanly curves. Tight underwear kept the chest flat, and drop waists hid the hips. Dresses, often in sheer fabrics, complemented dance moves: pleats gave freedom of movement, while fringing, beads, and tassels swayed with the beat.

During the daytime, the most fashionable young women wore comfortable twinsets (knitted tops and cardigans), like those designed by French couturier Coco Chanel. Chanel's clothes often had a nautical theme, and she popularized yachting

Luxury for All

Lace and silk had once been so expensive that they were available only to the very rich. Key producers of handmade lace included Italy, Belgium, France, England, Ireland, and China, but by the 1920s, cheap, machine-made lace was available. The twenties also saw the spread of artificial silk, or rayon. Although the first rayon plant had opened in the United States as early as 1910, the fabric really took off in the following decade. It was a popular choice for dresses and stockings.

trousers for women. The boyish look was completed with short-cropped, or bobbed, hair, worn under a bell-shaped cloche hat.

For those who could not afford couture, ready-made clothing was becoming more widely available in department stores, while cheaper sewing machines made it possible for ordinary women to copy some high-fashion styles at home.

A Passion for the Past

One of the most amazing archaeological discoveries of the twentieth century occurred in 1922, when Howard Carter opened Tutankhamun's tomb in Egypt's Valley of the Kings. This event influenced design of all kinds, including fashion. Egyptian-inspired textiles featured stylized lotus flowers or eye motifs. Popular colors included lapis lazuli (bright blue), sandy yellow, and papyrus green. Makeup, too, was heavy and black, like the dark kohl worn by ancient pharaohs and their queens.

Accessories

Showy costume jewelry was popular in the twenties, including enormous fake gems, known as paste or rhinestones. Long strings of pearls sat well on a boyish flat chest and swung about to emphasize energetic dance moves. Evening purses had tassels for the same reason. Smoking was taken up by the "fastest" young women and even this had its glamorous accessories—long,

Higher hemlines put women's footwear on display as never before. Popular styles included high-heeled T-bar shoes, and strapped shoes called Mary Janes.

jewel-encrusted cigarette holders, as well as slim cigarette cases and lighters.

The Great Gatsby

The look for fashionable young men during the twenties was captured in the fictional character of Jay Gatsby, created by the American author F. Scott Fitzgerald for his novel, *The Great Gatsby* (1925). Gatsby was wealthy, well connected, and dressed in lounge suits of pale linen, checked tweed, or soft, gray flannel.

The style for young men was relaxed. Suits had wide shoulders, roomy trousers, and modern zip flies instead of buttons. Informal shirts even had soft collars, instead of stiff, starched ones. Brogues were the usual footwear for daytime.

This dress by French couturier Paul Poiret was inspired by Ancient Egyptian style.

Leisure Pursuits

Knits and Tweeds

During the twenties it was fashionable to spend the weeks up in town, and the weekends in the country. Here, people pursued outdoor sports, including golf and cricket. Tweed plus-fours or knickerbockers were popular with male golfers. Plus-fours were so called because they ended four inches below the knee. Women sometimes wore knickerbockers, too, but tweed skirts were less controversial. These were worn with woolen sweaters. Britain's Duke of Windsor popularized the cozy Fair Isle sweater. Originating from one of the Shetland Islands in Scotland, Fair Isle knits feature a geometric pattern in soft colors.

Cream cricket sweaters, with a colored border stripe, also became popular leisure knitwear. Sleeveless sweaters were also worn, sometimes with the shirtsleeves underneath rolled up. Such casual styles were still worn with a hat. In summer, a light-colored straw panama was ideal. True panama hats were made in Ecuador. They could be squashed in a suitcase and still retain their shape.

On the Beach

Beach vacations and suntans were all part of the new, sporty lifestyle. France was the most chic European destination for the rich, who headed off to Le Touquet and Biarritz, or to exclusive resorts around the Riviera, such as Nice, Cannes, and Antibes. Many Americans headed to Europe, but those who stayed at home enjoyed the beaches of California and Miami. The middle and working classes also enjoyed seaside vacations. Each country had its own popular resorts—for example, Atlantic City and Ocean City in the United States, or Brighton and Blackpool in Britain.

Beachwear became a whole new area of fashion. For sunbathing and swimming, women wore all-in-one

A young woman in a bathing suit graces a shipping company poster. Contrasting stripes were popular for beachwear.

The Blue Funnel Line

Bronzed Beauties

In previous centuries, rich women had prized their pale skin, which showed that they lived a leisurely indoor life. Tans were a sign of being poor, and having to work outside in the sun. By the early twentieth century, however, the situation was reversed. Poorer women were more likely to work in a factory than out in the fields, and pale, wan skin became associated with poverty. Sunbathing became popular with the rich and the first suntan oils appeared.

costumes. Shaped like a tunic over long drawers, twenties' swimsuits seem modest today but at the time were daringly skimpy. Men, too, wore all-in-ones until the mid-twenties, when they adopted swimming trunks, which they wore with a tank top to cover the upper body. Costumes were made from cotton, wool, or silk jersey—and often shrank or stretched in the water! When they were not swimming, women covered up in comfortable, wide-legged "beach pajamas." At the time, trousers were still not generally worn by women.

Male golfers often paired their plus-fours with Fair Isle sweaters and socks. Sensible brogue shoes were worn by golfers of both sexes.

Chapter 4: The Thirties

After the high-living twenties, the thirties were a sober time. Following the Wall Street Crash (1929), economies slumped and the Great Depression took hold, with millions finding themselves unemployed. In the United States, Franklin D. Roosevelt's New Deal went some way toward providing help, but there was more trouble to come. Countries such as Germany and Japan began to build up their military power. The decade ended with the outbreak of World War II (1939–1945).

Fashion reflected the difficult times. Clothes were in subdued colors, such as black, gray, navy, and brown. Many families could not afford new clothes and managed with hand-me-downs. Designers responded to the depression by creating more ready-to-wear outfits in less costly fabrics, such as cotton and rayon.

New Fabrics

The thirties saw the appearance of more manmade fabrics, including artificial crêpe, improved rayon, and, by the end of the decade, nylon. Sanforizing was patented in the United States in 1930. Named for its inventor, Sanford L. Cluett, Sanforized fabric was preshrunk, which meant that clothes did not change shape after their first wash. Other innovative fabrics, such as Zingale, boasted that they were uncrushable.

Womanly Bias

The boyish figure was no longer fashionable. Hemlines dropped and dresses showed off female curves once more. Cloth was cut across the grain.

This technique, called bias cutting, used more fabric but produced flattering gowns, which had sweeping skirts but clung to the bosom and hips. Designer Alix (later known as Madame) Grès was especially skilled at creating bias-cut dresses that looked simple but elegant.

Short capes in plain fabrics suited daytime outfits. Gloves were an important accessory.

Twenties' styles had emphasized women's legs. During the thirties, hemlines swept the floor again and attention turned to the back. Backless evening gowns were the height of fashion.

Schiaparelli the Surrealist

One of the most outrageous designers of the decade was Italian-born Elsa Schiaparelli. She was linked with the Surrealists, a group of artists who produced fantastical images, often putting ordinary objects in surprising places. Schiaparelli used Surrealist ideas in fashion. She collaborated with Spanish artist Salvador Dali on her unusual hat designs, which were shaped to look like an upturned shoe, a lamb chop, an ice-cream cone, and a bird!

For those who could afford them, evening gowns were lavish. Made in flowing silks, satins, or rayon, they were often backless. Women wore little matching capes or bolero jackets, often trimmed with real fur.

Masculine Style

Not all women chose feminine dresses and skirts. Swedish actress Greta Garbo wore masculine tailored trousers with a belted trenchcoat and a beret. She also popularized the "slouch hat," after wearing it in *A Woman of Affairs* (1928). Created by the Hollywood dresser Adrian, this outsize cloche was pulled down over the forehead. It influenced hat design throughout the thirties.

Hollywood Hair and Cosmetics

The silver screen came to dominate fashion. Moviegoers copied the clothes and hairstyles of their favorite stars. Many bleached their hair with peroxide in order to look more like Jean Harlow, the platinum blonde who starred in *Bombshell* (1933). Others copied Greta Garbo's bob or Claudette Colbert's bangs.

Makeup, too, saw the influence of Hollywood, with women's magazines running step-by-step features on how to achieve filmstar glamor. Rouge and lipstick were essential items, and actress Joan Crawford's bright red lips were widely copied. Eyes were made up with cream or powder shadows, pencils, and brush-on mascara. Many women plucked their eyebrows into thin arches, like Marlene Dietrich's. The thirties also saw the appearance of false eyelashes and fingernails.

The flowing line created by bias-cut skirts and dresses emphasized the curves of the bust and hips.

Film star Greta Garbo was an inspiration to many women. Her slouch hat was widely copied.

Gangster Styles

During the years of Prohibition (1920–1933), when alcohol was banned in the United States, the black market flourished. Wealthy gangsters dressed in exaggerated versions of respectable business suits. The wide shoulders and narrow waists emphasized the torso, giving an impression of size, strength, and masculinity.

Designed for showing off, gangster suits came in eye-catching patterns, such as wide stripes or bold plaids. They were worn with colorful ties, two-tone shoes called spectator shoes, and colored felt fedora hats. During the thirties, the gangster look crossed over into mainstream fashion, with all men wearing wide-shouldered jackets.

Gangsters wore thick woolen overcoats with wide, contrasting lapels. Actor Edward G. Robinson played the typical Chicago gangster in *Little Caesar* (1931).

Early in the decade, male tennis players began to adopt shorts instead of long flannels.

Sports and Leisure Wear

On Vacation

In summertime, many men wore blazers, adapted from the sports jackets worn by nineteenth-century English university students. Blazers had shiny metal buttons and colorful stripes—originally used to identify teams—in blue, green, brown, cream, or buff, and were worn with linen slacks or shorts. Shorts were popular vacation wear, when they could be teamed with open-necked shirts and plain sweaters. Clothes were generally becoming more comfortable, with Lastex, a type of elastic, giving them a bit more stretch. Sunglasses, introduced fifty years earlier, became popular in the thirties.

Anyone for Tennis?

There was a great emphasis on health and fitness during the thirties. Tennis was one of the most fashionable sports. Male players began to wear shorts rather than long white flannels. The first to do so was Henry "Bunny" Austin at Forest Hills, New York, in 1932. Women players adopted shorts the following year. In 1933, a retired French tennis star, René Lacoste, set up his own clothing company. Nicknamed "the alligator" for his tenacity as a player, Lacoste designed sports shirts that had an embroidered crocodile logo—the earliest-known example of clothes with a logo designed to be seen.

Skiwear

Another sports craze was skiing, which had originated in Scandinavia but spread to other snowy, mountainous parts of the world in the early 1900s, including the United States. Skiers used wooden skis, attached to ordinary army boots with leather straps. Women skiers wore long trousers with cuffed hems and short, boxy jackets. Their cozy knitted sweaters often had ski-themed designs such as snowflakes or fir trees. Thick leather mitts were also worn, partly to protect the hands from rope burns, following the invention of rope tows to help skiers up the mountainside.

Swimwear

Around the mid-thirties, men stopped wearing their two-piece suits of trunks and tank tops and began to wear only trunks. At the same time, women adopted two-piece swimming costumes, which often plunged at the back. This allowed maximum exposure to the sun and ensured no tan marks when wearing a backless evening gown.

The Berlin Olympics

The sporting event of the decade was the Olympic Games hosted in Berlin, Germany, in 1936. German leader Adolf Hitler saw the Olympics as a chance to show off the fitness and superiority of the German, or "Aryan," race, but his hopes were dashed when African American Jesse Owens outperformed all the German athletes. Wearing leather shoes and a baggy shirt and shorts, Owens became the first-ever Olympian to win four gold medals. He also broke two world records.

Chapter 5: The Forties

In Britain, so-called Utility styles were mass produced. The suits, created by top designers of the day, followed strict guidelines regarding the use of rationed cloth.

The first half of the forties was dominated by World War II. The United States entered the war in 1941, following Japan's attack on Pearl Harbor. Peace finally came in 1945. Following the war, times remained hard. In Britain, clothes rationing continued until 1948 and food rationing until 1954. Nevertheless, peace brought a kind of optimism. Millions of babies were born—the "baby boomers"—as servicemen returned to their families. There was also a wave of hopefulness in fashion, epitomized by the extravagant "New Look."

Haute Couture in Hiding

During World War II, fashion took a back seat as all resources were needed for the war effort. Most women wore mass-produced, factory-made clothes in styles that used as little fabric as possible. As in World War I, women's fashions became more practical and took on a military look. Many more women began to wear trousers, which gave greater freedom of movement and eliminated the need to wear stockings, which were in short supply.

Rationing

Countries involved in the war introduced rationing to protect stocks of rare resources. Supplies of food, clothing, and furniture were all controlled. Rationing worked on a system of coupons, with a certain number of coupons being given up for different items of clothing. Everyone, rich or poor, received the same number of coupons. Clothes rationing began in the United Kingdom in 1941 and in the United States in 1942.

People found inventive ways to get the most from their clothes. Magazines ran articles suggesting how to adapt existing outfits. The fabric from a thirties' evening gown, for example, could go toward several new garments that used material more modestly. Government campaigns encouraged people to mend old clothes rather than throw them away. Finally, no coupons were required to buy secondhand clothes, so some people relied on others' cast-offs to add new life to their wardrobes.

Wartime Children

Clothing for children was also rationed. Families who were short of money sold their coupons on the black market in exchange for cash. Many boys and girls learned to knit, and outgrown sweaters were unwound so the wool could be reused. When Jewish children in concentration camps in German-occupied Europe outgrew or wore out their clothes, there were no replacements. Many went naked.

Norman Hartnell (1901–1979)

London-born Norman Hartnell showed his first collection in 1927. By 1938, he was official dressmaker to the British royal family. During the war, he began producing ready-to-wear clothes and also designed Utility clothing for the British Board of Trade (see page 24). In the 1950s, he designed Queen Elizabeth II's wedding and coronation gowns. Her wedding dress was made of white satin and embroidered with more than twenty thousand pearls.

Those children in hiding managed with whatever scraps of fabric their protectors could spare.

Occupied Paris

In June 1940, German soldiers marched into Paris, the fashion capital of the world. During the German occupation, over ninety French fashion houses were allowed to stay open, partly to dress the wives of high-ranking Nazi officers and also to bring in money from American customers. These fashion houses, which included Lucien Lelong, Jean Patou, and Pierre Balmain, were even allowed special fabric allowances.

Stage Costumes

Wartime entertainers did an important job of lifting people's spirits. They generally dressed in formal evening wear. Swing bands, for example, wore white tuxedos and black tie, while singers such as Vera Lynn wore long evening gowns. The styles of these clothes were unchanged from the designs of the thirties.

Swing music, or "big band" jazz, was popular from around 1935 to 1945. "King of Swing" Benny Goodman and his smartly dressed band entertained troops and civilians alike.

Designers play their part

In the United States and Britain, designers helped to produce civilian clothing that was versatile, hard wearing, and did not use scarce resources. The American plan was known as L85, because clothes used only eighty-five percent as much fabric. In Britain, the scheme was known as Utility clothing, and all garments bore the CC41 (Clothing Control 1941) label. Every aspect of the design of these clothes was controlled, down to the number of seams.

Working Women

Civilian women played a valuable role producing food on farms, working in factories, or running vital services such as buses and trains. All of these jobs required sensible clothes, such as overalls, jodphurs, or dungarees. Headscarves were a practical alternative to hats, as they kept hair clean and out of the way of machinery. Many women cut their hair, reducing the need for hairpins, which were in limited supply.

American pilots pose in leather A2 flight jackets. By the fifties, these were known as "bomber jackets," named for the wartime pilots who wore them.

Battle Dress

Men in Uniform

Servicemen wore their uniform all of the time, even on leave. Uniforms set them apart from ordinary civilians and were an outward sign that they were brave and fit to fight—even if they had been drafted. When the war ended, many had no clothes of their own and had to be issued with a "demob" (demobilization) suit for civilian wear.

World War II was fought in a variety of environments—from the chilly forests of northern Europe to the deserts of the Middle East. Each fighting nation produced a range of uniforms to suit the different forces—army, navy, air force, and so on—as well as different climates. Cool, light-colored cotton suits were worn by forces in the tropics, for example. Knitted cotton T-shirts were issued as undershirts to all American servicemen in the army and navy.

Forces' Coats and Jackets

Sailors in the British navy wore heavy woolen duffle coats, fastened with wooden "toggles." Duffle coats could be hip- or knee-length and some had a hood to keep off the rain. They became popular civilian wear after the war, when surplus coats were sold off. Another later fashion item was the A2 flight jacket, or battle jacket, issued to American pilots. Made of brown leather, A2 jackets first appeared in the early thirties, but are associated with World War II. Most were made of horsehide, but hard-wearing goatskin was also used; the wristlets were knitted wool. Although cockpits were no longer open to the elements, they could still be drafty and cold.

Women in Uniform

Women's uniforms were similar to men's, except they had skirts instead of trousers. Stitched-on badges indicated the wearer's rank. Most uniforms were in colors that offered good camouflage, such as khaki, olive green, or field gray. Some were the work of well-known designers. Mainbocher, the Chicago-born designer famous for his thirties evening gowns, was responsible for part of the Women's Red Cross uniform.

Nylons

Artificial nylon yarn first appeared in the United States at the end of the thirties. It proved a useful alternative to silk for making stockings—silk was in short supply as it was needed for making parachutes. Many American servicemen came to Europe with supplies of nylon stockings, which served as useful currency. However, even nylons were expensive and rare. Many women resorted to drawing stocking seams onto the backs of their bare legs!

American designer Mainbocher created various wartime uniforms, including this one, worn by the Navy Nurse Corps.

After the War

Curves and Corsets

When the war ended, designers experimented with several different styles, but none really captured people's imaginations—until the launch of Christian Dior's "Corolle" collection in February 1947. Soon known as the New Look, it was not really new at all, drawing inspiration from the styles of the thirties. However, it caused a stir because its full skirt required lavish quantities of fabric. At that time, clothes rationing had only just ended in the United States and was still in force in Britain. Some people declared that it was wasteful and unpatriotic to wear the new style, and there were even demonstrations on the streets.

Hostility to the New Look did not last long. Many women found its romance and femininity irresistible after years of drab, sensible clothing. They were even willing to wear tightly laced corsets again in order to achieve the necessary wasp waist. The "natural" silhouette also required softly rounded shoulder and hip pads, which helped to emphasize the body's curves.

Zoot Suits and Zazous

The shock value of using lots of fabric was not reserved for women's dress. In the early 1940s, African Americans and Mexican Americans had dressed in a new style of baggy suit known as the zoot suit. Zoot suits were ridiculously oversized and used reams of material. The long jacket had wide lapels and came down to mid-thigh or even as far as the knee. The wide-legged trousers had tight cuffs at the bottom to stop them from billowing out. Jazz musician Cab Calloway was one of the most famous zoot suit wearers. A similar style,

Seen here wearing a zoot suit, entertainer Cab Calloway was famous for being "togged to the bricks," meaning sharply dressed.

known as the *zazou*, arose in France around the same time.

Bathing Suits and Bikinis

During the war, two-piece swimsuits for women had become popular, chiefly because they used up less fabric. In 1946, a shocking version of the two-piece appeared, skimpier than any of its predecessors. The bikini was named after the remote Bikini Atoll in the Pacific Ocean, where the Americans carried out tests of atomic bombs between 1946 and 1958. The name was intended to suggest that wearing a bikini could

Christian Dior (1905–1957)

French designer Christian Dior began his fashion career aged thirty, selling catwalk sketches to newspapers. After working for designers Robert Piguet and Lucien Lelong, Dior opened his own couture house in 1947. His first collection, the New Look, sealed his reputation and made his fortune. For the next ten years, Dior was at the forefront of design, producing structured, feminine styles. He was also known for his accessories, such as pearl choker necklaces and wide-brimmed hats.

have explosive results! The bikini was launched by two French designers, Jacques Heim and Louis Reard.

Wartime Spin-Offs

Not all postwar advances in fashion set out to shock. Nylon had become a great success, and the late forties saw the appearance of more new fibers and fabrics, which had been developed during the war. The first polyester fiber, made from chemicals found in petroleum, was created in 1941 by British chemists working for ICI Ltd and patented under the name Terylene. During the Fifites, the American company DuPont went on to create more polyesters, including Dacron and Mylar. Like nylon, polyester was exciting because it was easy to care for, did not crease, and could be mass produced cheaply.

The nipped-in waists and full skirts of Dior's New Look seemed romantic and feminine after the sensible styles of the war years.

Left: The bikini, launched in the forties, became an enduring fashion fixture.

Chapter 6: The Fifties

During the fifties, post-war rivalry between the United States and the Soviet Union developed into deep mistrust, marking the start of a long period known as the Cold War. Its name came about because there was never direct military action between the two nations, although they took opposite sides in many conflicts around the world. The first of these was the Korean War (1950–1953), in which the United States backed the anti-communist south, while the Soviets supported communist North Korea.

Compared to the previous two decades, however, the fifties was a time of optimism and prosperity. Baby boomers born just after the war grew up to become the first "teenagers." Young people had their own fashions and culture, especially in the United States, which was the birthplace of rock and roll music.

There was an explosion of new technologies. Labor-saving appliances gave housewives more spare time. Invented in the twenties, television took off as sets became more affordable, and regular broadcasting began. Color television was available in the United States from 1953. The end of the decade saw a great advance, when the Soviets launched the first satellites into space.

Comfort and Practicality

Having emerged as a major superpower, the United States also took over in the world of fashion. Most everyday clothes were inspired by the "American look," mass-produced separates that could be mixed and matched. Twinsets—a sweater and matching cardigan—were very popular, usually in fresh pastel shades of pink, blue, and yellow. Sweaters were tight-fitting, as worn by the Hollywood "sweater girls," Marilyn Monroe, Lana Turner, and Jayne Mansfield. Some were made of wool, but others were in a new "wash-and-wear" blend of acrylic and cotton.

Skirts came to mid-calf, and could be straight or full. Pencil skirts were long

Bathing suits and beachwear from 1957. The fashionable fifties' silhouette had the bosom lifted and thrust forward in a pointed torpedo shape.

and straight and looked extremely elegant with a matching suit jacket and high-heeled shoes. Full skirts, a continuation of Dior's New Look, became exaggerated for the youth market. Worn over taffeta petticoats and sometimes featuring lots of accordion pleats, they permitted plenty of freedom for dancing.

Not everyone wore separates, however. The sack dress, introduced by Spanish designer Cristobal Balenciaga in 1956, was a carefully tailored but loose-fitting, knee-length dress that tapered in at the bottom. It provided a sharp contrast to the nipped-in waists of most fifties styles and was a forerunner of the sixties' shift dress.

Nylon and Elastic

Figure-hugging sweaters showed off the bosom, which was usually supported in a pointed "missile" bra. Synthetic fabrics revolutionized underwear. Bras and girdles were made from elastic and nylon, sometimes mixed with natural fibers. One of the decade's strangest inventions was the inflatable bra. Made of nylon and rayon, its cups had air pockets that could be blown up to achieve the desired bust size.

Fifties Fabrics

Although the fifties saw a revival of natural fabrics, such as cotton jersey and denim, nylon and polyester were everywhere! The new textiles took dye well, did not crease, and did not even get eaten by clothes moths. As well as continuing to develop new

Claire McCardell (1905–1958)

The most influential American designer of the fifties was Claire McCardell, who had begun to design clothes under her own label in 1940. She was known for her easy, sporty clothes and championed the use of simple, practical fabrics such as cotton, denim, gingham, calico, and even mattress ticking. In the forties, McCardell had created a wraparound denim dress called the "popover" and had paired her clothes with ballet-style pumps. In the fifties, her creations included comfortable two-piece playsuits for the beach, and peasant-style dirndl skirts.

fabrics, chemists found a way to permanently press material, resulting in lots of easy-care pleated skirts and dresses.

Nifty Suits

While America dominated womenswear, stylish men dressed in tailored suits from Italy. The Italian style featured a relatively short single-breasted jacket with tapered trousers. It was worn with a slim, horizontally striped tie and pointed leather shoes. Of course not everyone could afford to dress in the latest style of suit. In Britain, some men continued to wear the "demob" suits they had been given at the end of the war.

Cotton sundresses were printed with cheerful florals, checks, or stripes. Skirts were full, emphasizing the narrow waist.

Youth Styles

A group of beatniks read poetry together. Beatnik young women typically wore cropped capri pants or pedalpushers with sweaters or masculine-style shirts.

Brooding actor Marlon Brando was the epitome of the young rebel. In *The Wild One*, he played a motorcycle gang leader and wore a leather jacket, T-shirt, and tight-fitting jeans.

Hard-Working Materials

Blue–collar workers continued to dress in overalls and dungarees. Firefighters saw a huge improvement to their uniforms with the invention of aramid fibers, such as Kapton and Nomex. Aramids were a kind of fireproof nylon. As well as being used by firefighters, aramids were soon used to protect people in other professions, including racing drivers. Another invention of the fifties was Velcro, a method of fastening clothing inspired by the hooks on plant burrs.

Young Rebels

Work clothes became the uniform of the new generation of young, rebellious bikers, who adopted leather

jackets, jeans, and T-shirts. The look was captured on the silver screen by Marlon Brando in *The Wild One* (1953) and James Dean in *Rebel without a Cause* (1955). Jeans were invented by a Bavarian immigrant called Levi Strauss in the 1870s, and had originally been intended as workwear for Californian gold miners. They were made from strong cotton cloth called denim (originally from the French town of Nîmes) and were reinforced with metal rivets.

Beatniks

Another group of young rebels who emerged in the fifties were the Beat generation—poets and writers who hung out in the cafés of Paris, France, and Greenwich Village, New York. Although the beatniks, as they were known, did not want to conform in any way, their individual clothes style soon became a sort of uniform in itself. Many of the men grew goatie beards. Some wore plaid work shirts and jeans, while others slouched in shabby suits. Beatnik women dressed in pedalpushers and men's shirts, and sometimes cut their hair extremely short.

Cha Cha, Rock, and Jive

Dance crazes of the fifties had an enormous influence on youth styles. Rockabilly girls wore full, swirling skirts. Even their ponytails emphasized the twisting and twirling moves they made to the new rock and roll music. Boys wore snug-fitting jeans and two-tone shoes, just like their rock hero, Elvis Presley.

In Britain there were two main youth styles at the end of the fifties, which were as much defined by their musical tastes as by their clothes. The jazz-loving mods wore smart suits with tight, "drainpipe" trousers and short jackets. Those who could afford them rode Italian scooters, such as Lambrettas or Vespas. Rockers listened to rock and roll and dressed in scruffy jeans, T-shirts, and long, pointed shoes known as "winklepickers."

Hairstyles

During the fifties, more attention was focused on hair as hat wearing became less popular. Many women wore wigs or hairpieces so they could keep up with the latest styles, which could be short one season, then long the next. Hair dyes became more reliable from the middle of the decade. As well as covering gray hairs, they could also be used to introduce unnatural shades, such as pink or blue! There was also much more demand for hair products, such as shampoos, hair sprays, and pomades.

Chapter 7: The Sixties

The sixties were a time of enormous social change. Civil rights were a key issue and people campaigned to end discrimination on the basis of gender, color, sexuality, or class. There were serious race riots in Los Angeles (1965) and Detroit (1967), while the Stonewall Riots (New York, 1969) marked the start of the gay rights movement. In 1968, a student uprising in Paris, France, protested partly against the Vietnam War (1964–1975) and also demanded greater freedoms.

The sixties saw a sexual revolution. The oral contraceptive pill (1960) enabled women to experiment with sex without the fear of unwanted pregnancy. Sexual matters were also more openly discussed, and love scenes in books, films, and on television became more explicit.

Neat Suits

Many older women adopted elegant Chanel suits—or copies of these. Featuring a collarless cardigan jacket with a contrasting border and a knee-length skirt, the Chanel suit was comfortable and easy to wear. It was popularized by American first lady Jackie Kennedy, who wore hers with a small, oval hat, known as the pillbox.

Birth of the Mini

The youth fashion scene centered on London, where new designer boutiques stocked affordable clothes. Mary Quant was one of the first to produce miniskirts, but the mini also appeared in couture collections, for example by André Courrèges. Displaying more leg than ever before, the mini was an outward sign of women's new sexual freedom. Many of the older generation found it extremely shocking. Minis were often worn with knee-high boots, sometimes in PVC or Corfam (synthetic suede).

First popular in the twenties, the Chanel suit had a collarless tweed jacket with gilt buttons and matching skirt. It was typically worn with two-tone pumps and a pearl necklace.

Pierre Cardin was one of several designers inspired by astronauts' clothing. His oufits for men and women used unusual materials such as plastic and metal.

Hemlines fluctuated widely during the sixties. The mini stopped at mid-thigh, or even higher, but did not suit everyone. The midi skirt, which came to just below the knee, looked good on most women. The maxi came down to the ankle and suited taller physiques.

Art to Wear

Eye-catching patterns were another big story of the sixties. Many designers turned to high art for inspiration. In 1965, Yves Saint Laurent's famous "Mondrian" dresses borrowed the geometric, primary-colored paintings of abstract artist Piet Mondrian. Other designers drew from the popular op art movement, using textiles that created optical illusions, often in black and white.

Strange Materials

Another inspiration was the space race, with designers using synthetic modern materials in space-age silvers and whites. André Courrèges, Pierre Cardin, and Paco Rabanne were all known for their outrageous space-age styles. These designers worked in vinyl, synthetic rubber, and even metal, with Rabanne famously creating chainmail minidresses.

During the sixties, clothing for divers and surfers was revolutionized when Neoprene, a type of synthetic rubber, was adopted for wetsuits. Originally invented in the thirties, the material contained millions of air-filled bubbles, which meant that it did not become too heavy when wet, kept the wearer warm, and dried off very quickly.

Space Race

Between the late fifties and the seventies, the United States and Soviet Union competed in the exploration of space. At first, the Soviets were most successful. They launched the first satellite (1957), landed the first craft on the Moon (1959), and put the first human in space (1961). However, the biggest goal was to land people on the Moon. The Americans achieved this with the *Apollo 11* mission. On July 20, 1969, astronauts Neil Armstrong and Buzz Aldrin became the first humans to set foot on the Moon. Their spacesuits made a great impact on the fashion world—before long, people were wearing white suits, flat-heeled, knee-high white boots, and even visored helmets!

Hippie Chicks

The late sixties were dominated by a new youth movement, which originated around the Haight-Ashbury area of San Francisco. Hippies were young people who did not want to conform to establishment values. The name originally came from the term "hipster," meaning white people who were involved in "hip," black culture.

Hippies believed in free love and world peace. Many of them took recreational drugs, such as marijuana and LSD. They refused to follow their parents into "straight" jobs and they dressed to reflect their beliefs. Rather than giving money to big business, some preferred to make their own clothes. They knitted ponchos and sweaters in brightly colored wools and tie-dyed their own T-shirts. They gave clothes they had bought an individual touch by sewing on patches. They avoided synthetics, which were the products of big chemical companies, and favored natural fabrics instead, such as cotton, wool, and velvet.

Ethnic Styles

Many hippies adopted spiritual aspects of other cultures, such as Buddhism, Hinduism, or Native American religious beliefs. They also bought ethnic clothing, such as Indian peasant shirts, batik skirts, beaded vests, or the unisex kaftan. Kaftans were long, loose robes worn by desert nomads in North Africa and Asia. Since they covered up the body, they were especially popular with people who did not conform to the ideal sixties' body shape, which was tall and skinny. They were also extremely comfortable and easy to wear.

Psychedelic Suits

All hippies wanted to look different. Hippie men often just wore T-shirts and jeans, but in bright rainbow colors. Some wore suits, but these were nothing like the suits their fathers wore for work. They had outrageous patterns in loud checks or paisley swirls. Paisley was a decorative pattern inspired by Indian Mughal art. It was named for the town of

Popular with both sexes, kaftans came in wool, cotton, or even silk. They were often beautifully printed or embroidered.

Peaceful Protests?

Hippies tried to take on the establishment by peaceful means, but sometimes protests went wrong. The student riots in Paris in May 1968 turned nasty after uniformed police launched tear gas at the crowd. The most successful pacifist (peaceful) protests were probably the "Bed-Ins" staged by John Lennon and Yoko Ono, wearing just their pajamas. The first was held in the Amsterdam Hilton in the Netherlands. Lennon and Ono turned their honeymoon into an anti-war protest, spending a week in bed in front of the world's media. They later held another Bed-In in Montreal, Canada.

The Music Scene

Paisley, in Scotland, which developed a reputation for woven paisley-patterned shawls during the 1800s. Hippies teamed their suits with frilly shirts, worn open at the collar.

Vintage clothing was popular and some young men even dressed in old military uniforms, from World War II army surplus to the flamboyant styles of earlier centuries. For the cover of their album *Sergeant Pepper's Lonely Hearts Club Band* (1967), the Beatles wore long, candy-colored military coats, decorated with gold and silver braids, tassels, and badges of honor.

Pop stars had an enormous influence on the world of fashion. Young people dressed to look like the big names of the day, following the styles worn by the Beatles, the Rolling Stones, Bob Dylan, and Jimi Hendrix. The Beatles even had clothing named after them. Beatle boots were close-fitting with a cuban heel and pointed toe. They were worn with the Beatle suit, which had a collarless jacket and tight, drainpipe trousers.

The Beatles wore colorful military-style uniforms for the cover collage of Sergeant Pepper's Lonely Hearts Club Band, which was designed by British artist Peter Blake.

Hair, Makeup, and Jewelry

All Sorts of Hairstyles

The most famous hairdresser of the decade was Vidal Sassoon, whose clients included designer Mary Quant, model Jean Shrimpton, and film star Mia Farrow. Sassoon's first innovation was to reinvent the bob.

Some hippie men wore flamboyant, floral suits. The man in the foreground is wearing a jacket in a pattern called "Chrysanthemum", originally designed by William Morris in the 1870s.

Short, sleek, and dark, this made a big contrast to the backcombed fifties' beehives which were still being worn by older women. Boyish hairstyles such as the bob and crop harked back to the twenties, and hats from that era also saw a revival, with the reappearance of the cloche.

As the sixties progressed, hairstyles for both sexes grew longer and some young men grew beards. Women wore their long hair loose, or else in Native American-style braids. The Afro became a symbol of pride for black men and women and was also widely copied by non-blacks who had tight, frizzy perms that could be teased out with an Afro comb. Hippies wore a variety of headgear from floppy sunhats to bearskins and tall, pointed wizard hats. Berets and peaked caps were also popular for a while.

Making Up

Like all other aspects of sixties fashion, the makeup of the time was strong and eye-catching. At the beginning of the decade, the "dolly bird look" placed the emphasis on the eyes. Women created spidery lashes with thick coats of black mascara or stuck-on false eyelashes. They also used metal eyelash curlers to crimp the lashes. Eye shadow colors included bright blue, green, or space-age silver. The edges of the eyes were accented even more with a thick black liquid liner. By contrast, the look for lips was pale but shimmery. Lipsticks came in a wide range of sugary pinks, but the more

Makeup emphasized the eyes, with strong black outlines. Long hair was sometimes pinned up, in a softer version of the beehive.

adventurous chose colors such as silver, green, or white.

There was no single style of hippie make up. Some hippies did not use any cosmetics or beauty products, preferring to return to nature as much as possible, even tolerating body odor. Others used colorful cosmetic crayons to produce wild designs. Body painting was a popular pastime, especially at festivals. Swirling patterns, hearts, flowers, and slogans were all likely to appear on hippies' faces or bodies!

Cool Jewels

Just about every style of jewelry was popular at some time during the sixties. Op art minidresses suited bold necklaces of molded plastic, in black, white, or bold primary colors. Chanel-style suits were worn with chunky fake pearl chokers and other costume jewelry. Hippie accessories were often made of natural materials, such as wooden beads.

Pendants and Politics

Pendant necklaces became popular with all hippies, male and female. Pendants could be symbolic, and used to express political opinions or spiritual ideas. Popular designs included the ancient Egyptian ankh (a symbol meaning "life"); the Chinese sign for yin and yang (representing harmony); the sacred Hindu symbol, om (meaning cosmic unity); or, for pacifists, the CND (Campaign for Nuclear Disarmament) or "peace" symbol.

Chapter 8: The Seventies

The seventies was a time of great changes and social conflicts. The Vietnam War continued, despite demonstrations by anti-war protestors. There was a rise in more violent kinds of protest, with hijackings and terrorist bomb attacks. In 1972, Palestinian terrorists massacred the Israeli team attending the Munich Olympic Games.

There was an oil crisis (1973–1974), when Arab nations refused to sell oil to Israel's allies, leaving the United States and much of Western Europe with severe energy shortages. The Arabs were showing support for Egypt and Syria, Israel's opponents in the Yom Kippur War (1973).

Throughout the decade, unemployment rose and economies slumped. There were widespread strikes in the United Kingdom. In the United States, President Richard Nixon was forced to resign (1974), following the Watergate scandal. Glamorous or nostalgic fashions offered an escape from all of the social and political unrest. Other styles, such as punk, expressed people's frustration with society.

Retro Styles

The seventies saw designers revisiting styles from previous decades. Haute couture designers, such as Yves Saint Laurent, borrowed thirties' and forties' tailoring for their tweed suits and flowing evening gowns. Ralph Lauren drew inspiration from the clothes worn by settlers of the Wild West. His "Prairie" collection (1978) included calico and gingham frocks with ruffled hems.

In Britain, Laura Ashley produced inexpensive, flowery cotton dresses that looked home-sewn. With pintucks, ruffles, sashes, and lace trim, her garments harked back to around 1900. Many women assembled their own nostalgic look by visiting thrift shops. They mixed and matched

Jeans for all Pockets

Denim became more popular than ever. Over the decade, various styles were fashionable, from flared bell-bottoms to neat rollups. Tight-fitting jeans, decorated with sequins, were worn to the disco. Punks ripped their jeans and then fastened them back together with safety pins. At the end of the decade the first "designer jeans" appeared from Calvin Klein and Ralph Lauren. Jeans, originally valued because they were cheap and hard wearing, could now be shockingly expensive, depending on their label.

different styles—long, flowing skirts or baggy tweed trousers, austere lace blouses, or colorful, tight sweaters.

Work Clothes

Pantsuits were popular with women who were fighting for equality in the workplace, although A-line skirts were also worn. Trousers for men and women were generally flared and shirts had wide collars. Men wore wide, garish neckties, sometimes nicknamed "kipper ties," or even patterned silk cravats.

Hippie Hangovers

Flares were just one of the hippie fashions of the late sixties that began to influence the mainstream. Men wore their hair long and many grew beards or moustaches. Women, too, kept their hair around shoulder-length, styled with gentle waves or flips.

Ethnic clothing remained popular. As well as kaftans, some people wore a version of the *djellaba*, a North African hooded cloak. Cheesecloth smocks with embroidered yokes and full sleeves were adopted from eastern European folk costume.

Crazy Kimonos

A new generation of Japanese designers began to find success in the West during the seventies. They included Kenzo, Issey Miyake, Kansai Yamamoto, Yuki, and Rei Kawakubo. They created sculptural clothes in unusual fabrics, such as quilted satins or stiff silks. Many of their designs were inspired by traditional Japanese costume, including kimonos, sports clothes for judo and kendo, and even designs from traditional kabuki theater.

Bulletproof Vests

Police and soldiers gained a new level of protection with the introduction of bulletproof vests in the early seventies. They were made of Kevlar, an extremely strong and lightweight synthetic fiber that is also flame-resistant. Invented by DuPont chemist Stephanie Kwolek, Kevlar had been patented in 1966.

The crime-fighting trio who starred in TV's *Charlie's Angels* wore wide-lapelled pantsuits and shirts with big collars. Their hair was fashionably long, with flips and waves.

Japanese designer Yuki opened his own company in 1973. He became famous for his long, draped jersey dresses.

Left: Designers such as Ralph Lauren and Laura Ashley tapped into people's nostalgia for simple, turn-of-the-century styles.

Sports and Leisure

Working Out

The fastest-growing area of fashion in the seventies was sportswear. Suddenly everyone was getting fit and needed exercise clothes. A tennis boom thrust players such as American Chris Evert and Swede Björn Borg into the limelight. Adidas tennis shoes and Slazenger or Head sweat bands were seen on the street as well as on the tennis court.

Interest in aerobics and dance helped to popularize leotards and legwarmers, while joggers bought up the new ranges of tracksuits and running shoes. These were in comfortable, stretchy fabrics, such as velour or terry.

Not all disco-goers felt comfortable in body stockings. Some male dancers strutted their stuff in three-piece suits, like the one worn by John Travolta in *Saturday Night Fever* (1977).

On the Dancefloor

Keep-fit clothing was designed with freedom of movement in mind, so it made sense to adopt similar styles for the disco. Discothèques became popular in the United States toward the end of the seventies, and the craze soon spread. Under flashing lights and mirror balls, young people danced and posed in lurex and satin. Clingy body stockings, tiny hotpants, and sequinned "boob tubes" showed off their exercised bodies. Top designers produced their own disco outfits. American Roy Halston, for example, was famous for his jumpsuits and halter-top dresses.

Super-Stretchy!

Spandex was invented as early as 1959. During the seventies, under the trademark Lycra, it started to appear in sports and disco outfits, as well as underwear. Adding Lycra to a material such as cotton gave stretch and helped the fabric keep its shape. Lycra was also quick drying, which was an advantage for sports or dancing.

Lycra breathed new life into other synthetics such as rayon, nylon, and polyester, which were being used for the nostalgic fashions. Lamé, a twenties' brocaded cloth with tinselly metallic threads, also reappeared with stretchy Lycra added.

One of the most outrageous fashion fabrics of the decade was fake fur. Wearing real fur was becoming unacceptable to some people, concerned about animal welfare. Fake

Skateboarding

Originally known as "sidewalk surfing," skateboarding began with people riding surfboard-shaped boards set on wheels. The first manufactured skateboards appeared in 1965, and by the seventies skateboarding was a craze. The first skate parks opened in the United States. Skateboard riders developed their own fashion style, wearing baseball caps, T-shirts, and baggy jeans. The sport started to decline in the early eighties, with the arrival of BMX bikes and rollerskates, but saw a revival in the nineties.

fur was a fun alternative. It was made to look obviously fake, so no one could mistake it for the real thing. Leopard spots and tiger stripes were the most popular fake fur prints.

Weatherproof Coats

The seventies also saw the appearance of sporty outerwear. Most people had a lightweight, rainproof nylon anorak that folded up into its own pocket. Windproof parkas with cozy fur-lined hoods were also popular. Knitted helmets called balaclavas were often worn by schoolboys for extra warmth in winter.

Left: With its cozy, fur-lined hood, the parka was based on the warm, sealskin jackets worn by Inuits in the far north.

Decade of Protest

Youth Styles

Like the sixties, the seventies was a time of social protest. Groups that had traditionally been marginalized by society—including women, blacks, and gays—continued to fight for their rights. The peace movement grew stronger, with largescale campaigns against the Vietnam War and the growing nuclear threat. There was also an increasing awareness of environmental concerns. Unlike sixties' protestors, those of the seventies sometimes resorted to violence, such as sieges or letter bombs.

Anti-War Clothes

Strangely, anti-war protestors often adopted military clothes. They bought army surplus because it was cheap and practical. The clothes, in khaki or camouflage prints, did not show the dirt, and were hard wearing. Combat trousers and jackets also had plenty of useful pockets. More importantly, protestors wore uniforms to show that they were at war—with the establishment. They also wore it to undermine the real soldiers.

Gay Rights

Homosexuals came up with their own "uniform." Gay men looked to "manly" styles, including dungarees and leather, which they adapted in order to flaunt their sexuality. The workman's white string undershirt, for example, became a raunchy undershirt in black fishnet. Fetish clothing, such as chains and studs, was also popular. Gay women, too, dressed to express their sexuality. Rather than conforming to how men liked to see women, some lesbians shaved off their hair, threw out their makeup, and wore macho denim dungarees.

Black Panthers

The Black Panther Party was founded in 1966 to fight for black equality. Members rejected the peaceful politics of people like Martin Luther King Jr., who had wanted blacks and whites to live side by side. Instead they wanted the right to determine their own communities, and dispense their own justice. In the early seventies the Panthers fell apart, but splinter groups emerged. To show they meant business, black activists adopted a kind of uniform. They wore military-style berets with black leather jackets, turtleneck sweaters, and black jeans.

Hair

Hairstyles also became a badge of

identity for other groups. Black men and women continued to adopt the Afro as a symbol of black pride. Anti-war protestors generally wore their hair long, not just because they were hippies, but also to contrast with the cropped hair of the soldiers they opposed. Toward the end of the decade, new styles appeared. Glam rockers teased their hair into larger-than-life styles. Spiky punk haircuts, often dyed in primary colors, were even more shocking.

Music Scenes

Glam rock had its roots in the New York scene around artist Andy Warhol. It was a glamorous, stagy, and feminine look for men. They wore tight, glittering clothes with feather boas and tall platform-soled boots, as well as lots of make-up—rouge, eye shadow, and lipstick. One of the most prominent glam rockers was David Bowie, who reinvented his look several times during the decade. Few ordinary people adopted the glam look.

Punk was another style that was seen on-stage, but also spread to the streets. It emerged in London and New York around the late seventies. Punks were rebelling against middle-class values. They wore ripped T-shirts, tight leather trousers, combat boots, and bondage jewelry. They distressed their clothing themselves, and painted slogans onto their leather jackets. Body piercings were also part of the look, with rows of studs, rings, or even safety pins through the ears, nose, or eyebrows.

Sid Vicious, bass player in British punk band the Sex Pistols, was one of the seventies' most notorious figures. His story was told in the film *Sid and Nancy* (1986), as played by Gary Oldman, above.

Chapter 9: The Eighties

The eighties saw the end of labor union influence in politics, and the rise of a riskier, more individualistic, free market culture. Fashion changed to reflect the "greed is good," ambitious attitude. Some clothes expressed this desire to seem successful, while others were a deliberate rejection of those values.

Young adults in the eighties wanted high-powered, highly paid jobs. People in their twenties had more money to spend on consumer luxuries than ever before, and their tastes set the trend for the fashion market.

Western governments focused on winning the Cold War with the Soviet Union, which US president Ronald Reagan called "the evil empire." Some eighties designers used symbols from the West's enemy, such as a crossed hammer and sickle, or a red five-pointed star, to communicate "rebel" values. The Soviet Union began to collapse in 1989, with the fall of the Berlin Wall.

Power Dressing

As in the twenties and thirties, men's suits stiffened to create a triangular frame, with wide shoulders and a fitted, narrow waist. This powerful look was emphasized with very dark grey flannel materials and expensive details, such as silk linings. Names like Armani, Gucci, Ralph Lauren, and Calvin Klein became global fashion brands.

Women's suits also widened at the shoulders, which were built up with shoulder pads, while skirts shortened. Hair was worn fluffed out, as "big hair." Makeup became bolder and used a wider palette of colors. The result was more powerful and predatory. This look was popularized in television soap operas, in the glamorous costumes worn by *Dallas's* Sue Ellen Ewing (played by Linda

Power-dressing women often favored mismatched jackets and skirts. Here a houndtooth check jacket with shoulder pads and a wide belt was paired with a leather-look skirt.

Supermodels

As consumer wealth increased, more fashion magazines appeared, and it became harder for fashion designers to make headlines in all of them. They needed the help of a celebrity model, who could guarantee coverage by magazines around the world. The eighties saw the emergence of supermodels, including Claudia Schiffer, Naomi Campbell, and Cindy Crawford. Many became so famous that they would soon sell their own fashion and beauty products.

Gray), and *Dynasty*'s Alexis Carrington Colby (played by Joan Collins) and Krystle Carrington (played by Linda Evans).

Glamorous Evening Wear

Women's evening wear was more dramatic than the style for daytime clothing. Gianni Versace used shocking, garish fabrics and exciting peepholes or slashes in clothing. Designers such as Oscar de la Renta and Karl Lagerfeld provided more classic evening styles, with sleek, draping fabrics and glittering details such as sequins.

Yuppie Accessories

Young, upwardly-mobile professionals (known as yuppies) spent their new wealth on gadgets and other accessories. Expensive brands of sunglasses, such as Ray-Bans, became an important symbol of yuppiedom. Yuppies also sported the first mobile phones, status symbols which came attached to a briefcase full of batteries and electronics.

High-Fashion Watches

The Swatch wristwatch was the accessory success story of the eighties. Launched in 1983, it was fun and affordable and came in colors and designs to match—or clash with—every outfit. For the first time, consumers purchased more than one watch. Initially bought only by teenagers, Swatches became highly collectable, especially the limited edition watches designed by world-class artists such as Keith Haring.

New Man

For men who were critical of macho culture, power dressing was a turnoff. The "New Man" preferred soft fabrics, romantic or floppy tailoring, and pastel colors. Even in a suit, New Man wanted to look as though he might have just stepped off the beach, wearing his shirt open at the neck, and shoes without socks.

Drama from Japan

As design and detail became increasingly important to the discerning consumer, Japanese expertise with texture and fabric became a must-have. First recognized in the seventies, designers Issey Miyake, Kenzo, and Yohji Yamamoto won the loyalty of many American and European consumers.

Don Johnson, star of the TV series *Miami Vice*, wore double-breasted designer suits in a casual way, often teaming them with a rumpled T-shirt.

The Gap

American clothing stormed the international stage in the late eighties with the rapid rise of labels and retailers such as the Gap. The Gap brought a hint of designer label within the reach of the average shopper's budget. In 1983, the Gap hired Millard Drexler to develop their appeal. His simple, bright, inexpensive fashion items, using good-quality textiles, grabbed the public's attention, eventually making the Gap the second largest clothing retailer in the world.

Jeans, the Gap's mainstay, were big business in the eighties. The decade saw the relaunch of the classic Levi 501s with a massive advertising campaign. Exclusive designers also brought out jeans, which were highly priced and highly sought after for their "designer label" on the back pocket. Giorgio Armani led the way with Armani Jeans, launched in 1981.

Big Brands

Some manufacturers' brands—their names and corporate logos—began to be used in street fashions as a badge of belonging to an in-crowd. Sports shoe makers Nike and Adidas grew from specialist sports manufacturers to the huge global brands they remain today. Branding was also vital for designers such as Calvin Klein, whose male underwear had his name embroidered onto the waistband, making underwear a design statement.

More traditional high-fashion labels, such as Chanel, began to seem a bit stuffy compared to these hard-edged brands. Punk designer Karl Lagerfeld was hired by Chanel in 1983 to bring in younger, funkier clients for the label. His designs won back Chanel's chic reputation.

Sporty Styles

Dancewear

The disco fever of the late seventies developed into dancing as a kind of sport, as expressed in the influential movies *Flashdance* (1983) and *Footloose* (1984). A "rehearsing ballerina" look became popular, with figure-hugging leotards and tubular woolen socks without feet, called legwarmers. Other sports-related fashion details included sweatbands and vibrant, neon-colored flashes and stripes.

Rollerskating in the park was a popular way to keep fit in the city. A bodysuit and headband gave this rollerskater a sporty look.

Sports Casual

Concern for health and fitness grew in the eighties, becoming a badge of self-respect and ambition. Casual clothing expressed this desire to look good and to seem fit and powerful. Tracksuits made people look like they might be about to go jogging. Leggings stretched taut from a loop under the heel suggested that the wearer could be on her way to a session at the gym. This clothing was not only fashionable, but also very comfortable—ideal for going shopping or watching television.

Pop Styles

MTV, the music television channel launched in 1981, connected young music consumers in many countries with the biggest pop idols. Short video films alongside a song made it easier for fans to copy the fashion styles of their favorite musicians. Stars such as Madonna changed global trends by appearing on MTV in unexpected clothing. Madonna's outfits made their designer Jean-Paul Gaultier even more famous. Hip-hop artists also had a big influence, driving sales of athletic shoes around the world.

Techno Fabrics

A new textile, Gore-Tex®, was patented in 1978, making sports clothing in the eighties far more appealing to men. Male consumers tend to appreciate high-tech functions in clothing, and Gore-Tex® offered the amazing power to repel water from outside the clothing, while allowing sweat to evaporate from inside. Following this breakthrough, manufacturers developed other new fabrics, such as flame-proof, unrippable, or even chainsaw-proof textiles. These advanced fabrics, often brightly colored, made for striking winter coat styles.

Left: Gore-Tex® was especially popular with walkers and climbers. It was used for jackets and pants that protected against wind and rain.

Chapter 10: The Nineties

At the beginning of the nineties the Cold War finally ended, with the breakup of the Soviet Union. In 1991, American president George Bush announced a "new world order," where nations would work together to end war and poverty. But the nineties were a decade of instability, with countries and federations breaking up, sometimes violently.

With his scruffy hair and baggy old sweaters, Nirvana's lead singer Kurt Cobain was the "king of grunge." Cobain committed suicide in 1994.

Fashion design expressed a similar mood of chaos and disintegration. Many young people adopted anti–fashion "grunge" styles, wearing clothes that deliberately looked dirty and scruffy. The grunge look was associated with the rock band Nirvana, and was expressed on the catwalk by designers such as Marc Jacobs and Martin Margiela.
The traditional divide between high

Fashion Without Cruelty

Fur was driven out of fashion by campaigns for animal welfare in the late eighties and early nineties. PETA (People for the Ethical Treatment of Animals) ran a high-profile campaign in 1993 involving models such as Naomi Campbell. By the decade's end, though, fur was back. Campbell herself left PETA in 1997, having decided that if leather, suede, and meat eating were okay, then fur should be too. The century ended with a brief fur revival on the catwalks.

fashion and mass consumption blurred. Department stores employed cutting-edge designers to create cheap, "fashion-forward" items. Fashion-conscious teens, meanwhile, turned to secondhand stores to build their own retro styles.

In a decade lacking strong social trends and ideas, many fashion consumers wanted clothing with meaning. Eco-friendly features, or little ethnic details such as embroidery, made the wearer feel that their clothing made a difference to other people's lives or to the environment.

Pure New World

In 1990, designer Rifat Ozbek presented an all-white collection to an amazed public. Ozbek wanted to get back to basics in his own work, but the collection had a wider influence, seeming to suggest that purity and simplicity were the next big things. The trend grew strong enough to provoke counter currents in nineties fashion: grungy, traditional, or busy and colorful.

Magpie Fashions

If the nineties had a unifying theme, it was that the unifying theme was dead. Instead of the top-to-toe look created by one design house and then widely copied, fashion now demanded that designers and consumers alike mixed and matched items of clothing, footwear, accessories, and hairstyles. Influences from across the decades, and from many different cultures, were combined to create unexpected new fashion statements. Elements from every postwar decade were revisited, including the platform shoes and punk hairstyles of the seventies.

Unisex

As eighties' macho values went out of style, tough new tomboy ideas of femininity emerged. Young women adopted camouflaged combat pants and hefty workboots. The early nineties' comic series *Tank Girl*, and the *Tomb Raider* game character Lara Croft (1996), were figureheads of this trend. Tattooing and body piercing became more widespread. Other androgynous fashions included shaved heads for women, and sarong skirts for men.

Nineties' Glamor

Some designers made womenswear that was more openly sexual. Bras, corsets, garters, and other underwear were now worn as outerwear. Clothes had revealing holes scissored through them. On some catwalks, flimsy dresses—sometimes held up only by dabs of glue on the skin— looked as if they were about to fall off and reveal a naked body!

Nineties' computer game character Lara Croft wore sleek, sexy outfits but had the weapons and training to fight hard and dirty. Angelina Jolie played Lara in the *Tomb Raider* films.

Heatproof Clothing

The end of the nineties saw new developments in heatproof clothing. NASA designers used their spacesuit expertise to improve the suits worn by terrestrial firefighters. Their aluminium-and-Kevlar-coated fire-resistant suits had a special cooling capacity.

A new material called CoolTek was also developed. CoolTek garments have three layers: a breathable outer shell, a layer of water-absorbent fibers, and a layer that conducts heat. The garment is soaked in water for a few minutes, and then the water slowly evaporates, keeping the wearer cool for hours. CoolTek clothing was adopted by people working in very hot environments, such as foundry workers, pilots, and firefighters.

In 2000, Speedo developed Fastskin, a revolutionary new swimsuit material based on sharkskin. Fastskin FSII, shown here, appeared four years later.

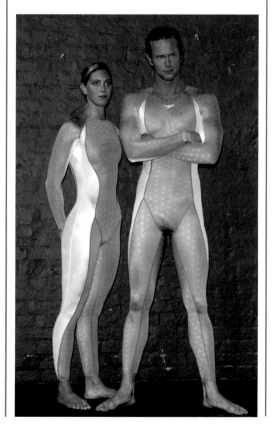

Sporting Fashions

Eighties' sports clothing had been designed to show off a fit, muscular body; by contrast, nineties' sports fashion trends were associated with "slacker" sports such as skateboarding, snowboarding, and surfing. ("Slacker" was the name given to a new generation of dropouts who were reacting against the go-getting culture of the previous decade.) Baggy jeans, beaten-up sneakers or basketball shoes, and loose tops were accessorized with bangles, ethnic necklaces, and tattoos. Australian clothing labels such as Billabong and Mambo made an impact on the world fashion scene.

In the Swim

Low-drag swimwear technology changed throughout the nineties, with the introduction of new fabrics and suit styles. Speedo's S2000 (1992), Aquablade (1996), and Fastskin (2000) were widely adopted by swim athletes, promising increased ability to slice through water. These fabrics mimicked the pattern of rough and smooth scales on the skin of a shark.

High-Performance Fabrics

Hooded tops in cozy fleece fabrics were popular with adults and children of both sexes. Polartec was an innovative fleece made from recycled plastic bottles. It was soft and warm, but also dried quickly if it got wet. Another new, eco-friendly material was Lyocell, first made in

1992 out of renewable wood pulp. Lyocell was manufactured under various trade names, including Tencel, which was used for figure-hugging tops, dresses, and underwear. Depending on the production process, Lyocell could be made to feel like silk, leather, or suede.

Dressing for War

The nineties was a decade of conflicts, from the invasion of Panama (1989–1990) to the civil wars in former Yugoslavia (1991–1995 and 1998–1999). Media images of soldiers in combat inevitably inspired some fashion items. New styles of aviator sunglasses and combat trousers with blue-pattern camouflage both took a turn as "hot" fashion items. The first Gulf War (1991) also inspired a Yellow Ribbon campaign. Some Americans and Britons wore yellow ribbons or tied them to trees, as a sign that they were awaiting the safe return of their troops.

Uniforms worn in the first Gulf War addressed the problems of the heat, dust, and oil, as well as the risk of chemical weapons. Soldiers wore anti-radiation suits and masks when investigating targets such as tanks. To protect against biological weapons, uniforms were soaked in pesticides, although these may have brought their own set of health risks.

U.S. soldiers serving in the first Gulf War wore uniforms designed to provide camouflage in the desert, and some protection against the extremes of heat and cold.

Strange Materials
The nineties saw a high-tech revival of the sixties' fashion for clothes in unusual materials, such as metals, paper, and plastics. Some designers created evening gowns and wedding dresses in fine-spun metal fabrics, such as aluminium. British designer Hussein Chalayan's "cast dresses" were made from hinged panels of rigid, molded polyester resin. Chalayan also used Tyvek, a papery material commonly used for envelopes. Developed as early as 1955, Tyvek is also used for the protective clothing worn in hospitals. It is strong, lightweight, and water-resistant.

Chapter 11: Costume Around the World

From 1900 onward, fashionable clothing became more accessible to a greater number of people around the world. Higher living standards enabled less wealthy people to buy clothes for pleasure, not just as a practical necessity. Advances in transportation and communications led to closer global ties, and the emergence of international brands and fashions. More people moved out of the countryside into cities. Cities grew, and city life changed how people dressed. Traditional costume fell out of favor.

Then, toward the end of the century, many people began to feel that global fashions made the world too boring and similar. Traditional costumes became appealing again, because they were unique to one place or cultural tradition. They expressed the special identity of their wearer, something that could not be copied endlessly around the world.

At a personal level, traditional costumes gave people a sense of security and belonging in a big and busy world. They also provided economic benefits for small communities, because they encouraged interest from tourists, who were eager to see and buy unique and traditionally crafted clothing.

Aboriginal Costumes

From the seventies onward, Australian aboriginals began to revive the cultural practices of their ancestors, which had been disappearing since Europeans began to colonize the land in the nineteenth century. They also recreated simple costumes of body paint, feathers, and natural materials. In part, costumes were used to confirm and celebrate their membership in a unique cultural tradition. They were also displayed as a tourist attraction, with tourists paying to view rituals and to photograph costumes.

Bones and Feathers

In warm or tropical places, traditional costume often consisted simply of

New Materials

In Papua New Guinea, tribespeople have incorporated modern, global products into their traditional costume. In the Western Highlands, for example, Johnson and Johnson's Baby Powder is daubed on as body decoration instead of clay. Elsewhere, it is thrown over dancers in place of crushed seashells, rubbed into female mourners' bodies, or used to purify corpses.

Real fur is still worn by Inuits living in northwestern Canada, to give protection against the biting cold.

belts to help carry things, and some jewelry. For example, the Zoe Indians of Brazil wore a bone through the lower lip as children, replaced with a wooden spike as adults. On special occasions, strips of bark and strings of feathers were stuck to the body with gum.

The Far North

Peoples living within the Arctic Circle, such as the Inuit, Sami, and Chukchi people, had an important reason for preferring traditional costume to fashion clothing. The climate is too cold and hazardous to risk using clothing that has not been tested for Arctic survival. A few new clothing technologies, such as Gore-Tex®, passed these tests, but fur boots and fur trousers remained unbeatable for daily life. Hunting, skinning, and sewing fur clothing had the added advantage of relying on local expertise, so local economies benefited.

Mountain Dress

Peoples of high pastureland and mountains across the world had similar survival needs, and relied on the same limited resources. Wool remained the main material for costumes in places as far apart as the Andes mountain range of South America and the highlands of Tibet in Central Asia. Andean and Tibetan peoples made wool into brightly colored, warm clothing, just as they had for centuries. They tinted plain wool with colors from roots, seeds, bark, beetles, and many other sources.

Porters at a campsite near Machu Picchu on the Inca Trail in Peru, wearing traditional, colorful ponchos woven from llama and alpaca wool.

Preserving Customs

From the fifties onward, faster shipping allowed people to manufacture clothing in any part of the world, while keeping costs down. Jet aircraft also made it easier for people and goods to move around the globe. Globalization made it harder for traditional cultural practices, including clothing, to survive. It gave young people more choice, beyond what their elders offered from tradition. However, in another way, globalization also helped to reinforce tradition by bringing wealthy tourists to poor areas, wanting to experience traditional local culture.

Traditional Native American costume is still worn on special occasions, such as this annual Pueblo Pow Wow in Taos, New Mexico.

Costume was sometimes only worn for special occasions, in order to maintain a cultural tradition. The Zulu peoples of southern Africa live and work as farmers, miners, or city workers. However, for ritual occasions they adopted the clothing of their warrior ancestors: a goatskin apron, leather shield, and accessories which would once have demonstrated a warrior's bravery—headgear and necklaces made from the hides and claws of dangerous animals.

Kente Cloth

Kente cloth is woven by the Asante peoples of West Africa. It is brightly colored, with powerful geometric designs. It was originally worn only by Asante kings, but gradually came to be worn by everyone as a costume for special occasions and even as everyday clothing. Kente cloth also became a symbol of pride for African Americans, worn for the winter festival of Kwanzaa.

Pow-wows

From the seventies onward, a movement grew to preserve Native American culture, including traditional clothing such as beaded skin tunics and trousers, or leather moccasins. At pow-wows, clan gatherings, and celebrations, full costume sometimes included eagle-feather "war bonnets" or headdresses. Even those Native Americans who wore Western dress often retained traditional hairstyles such as braids, and accessories such as beaded buckskin bags.

National Dress

Traditional clothing from one region of a country might be adopted as a "national dress," a costume for anyone to wear to express loyalty to the nation. National dress fell out of use in most European countries in the twentieth century, being worn only in historical reenactments, or as entertainment for tourists.

Japanese Kimono

The kimono is a formal Japanese robe, worn by men and women. Its wide sleeves and flowing folds have been part of Japanese courtly life for twelve hundred years, following a Chinese design which is itself over two thousand years old. During the twentieth century, Japanese people wore kimonos for special events such as weddings or the Children's Day festival.

There are at least seven different styles of kimono, expressing different degrees of formality. Putting them on correctly was such a complex process that licensed kimono dressers could be hired to help women prepare for the most formal events.

Revolutionary Clothing

The People's Republic of China was founded in 1949, under the leadership of Chairman Mao. In this new communist state, people adopted a kind of uniform that expressed their social equality. Made of dark, heavy-duty cotton, the practical "Mao suit," or *zhifu*, could withstand the rigors of hard labor. Both jacket and trousers were comfortable and loose-fitting, and the military jacket had four

Traditionally made in stiff silk, kimonos usually feature a striking repeat pattern. This kimono was designed in 1973.

roomy pockets and a turn-down collar. The Mao suit was worn by everyone, male or female, from government officials to farm laborers.

Mao's regime banned the cheongsam, or *quipao*, a figure-hugging, beautifully decorated dress, fastened with a line of cloth-covered buttons running from the neck diagonally across the front of the right shoulder. Although it had roots in the seventeenth century, its shape evolved throughout the twentieth century, acquiring shorter sleeves and a more fitted line. After fifty years "in exile," the cheongsam became popular again at the end of the century, especially as a cocktail dress.

Comfortable and hard-wearing, the Mao suit was a practical style of dress for workers of all kinds in communist China.

Famous Hats

Many local cultures are associated with a particular type of headgear. North African countries such as Morocco and Egypt are home to the fez, a small, red felt cylinder with a black tassel, worn high on the head. Wide-brimmed hats to shield farmers working in the hot sun include the Mexican sombrero and the "coolie" hats worn by rice farmers in Southeast Asia.

Religious Costumes

Costume has always been especially important in religious rituals. It reminded the participants that their activities were sacred. Special robes for leaders of ceremonies marked them out as the focus of the ritual. As a community's religious leader retired, their robes were often passed to their successor.

Costume Colors

Many religions treat certain colors as significant. The earliest-known religious rituals used ocher, a red pigment, probably as a symbol for blood. In Hindu and Shinto religions, white is associated with death. Buddhists may wear saffron-colored robes, symbolizing their rejection of worldly desires. Purples and blacks feature in the religions of Judaism, Christianity, and Islam as signs of God's power and authority.

Jewish Dress

Throughout the twentieth century,

some schools of Judaism wore traditional costume in their daily lives. The *kippa*, or *yarmulka*, is a tiny round cap worn on the crown of the head as a sign of respect for God. The *tallit*, a shawl with tasseled corners, is used during morning prayer—the tassels are reminders of God's commandments.

Christian Costumes

Different branches of Christianity used very different costumes. Orthodox Christian priests, especially in Greece and Russia, often wore pointed, cylindrical, and mitered (double-peaked) hats. Many Roman Catholics used a string of beads called a rosary to count how many times they have said a prayer. During the twentieth century, some Protestant Christian priests began to wear everyday clothes with a "dog collar"—a white band of material across the neck—in the place of a necktie.

At a traditional Greek Orthodox wedding, the bride and groom wear crowns to symbolize the marriage.

One Christian community, the Amish, tried to dress according to the rules of the old Hebrew Bible. Amish men wore plain-colored clothes and simple broad-brimmed hats. The women wore plain full dresses and aprons. Makeup, hairstyling, and details such as buttons were not allowed by many Amish. This helped them to remember that their first duty was always to God, not to themselves.

Muslim Dress

The Koran gives Muslim men and women guidance on dress. Islamic costumes varied according to which interpretations of Islam a community followed. Women's clothes were designed to conceal the female form, for modesty. The *chador*, for example, was a black robe that draped over the whole body, with just a small gap for the eyes to see through. The *burka* was a similar garment that covered the face, upper body, and arms—its eye slit was usually filled with embroidered net. Other Muslim women wore a *hijab*, a headscarf. The *jilbab* was a long shirt dress which covered the body but revealed the head and hands.

Religious Hairstyles

Some religions set rules for how the hair should be worn. Many Muslim, Jewish, and Amish communities expected men to have a beard—as they had for centuries. Sikh men never cut their head hair, wearing it coiled up inside a turban. Rastafarians also never cut their hair, letting it grow into matted "dreadlocks." Some Christian and Buddhist monks had shaven heads, while Hindu pilgrims in Madras, India, sacrificed their hair to the god Vishnu.

These Muslim women, photographed in Uzbekistan in 1992, each wear a form of headcovering, or *hijab*.

Muslin Masks

One religion required its monks and nuns to wear a veil of muslin over their mouths, not for modesty, but as part of their practice of Ahimsa, or "avoiding harm." Jains believed that all life-forms are equal and that harming another creature must be avoided at all costs. Monks and nuns wore the muslin mask or veil to prevent accidental harm by breathing in flying insects. For the same reason, they carried a broom and swept the ground ahead of where they trod, in order to clear any insects out of the way.

Pomp and Circumstance

Communities sometimes needed special clothing for rituals and traditions which had nothing to do with religion—for example, to mark an important national holiday. The more important and serious the occasion, the more formal the costumes. In the United States, the tuxedo jacket was worn by civilian men to formal dinners from the twenties onwards and became the standard formal dress for men in many parts of the world.

Parade Dress

National celebrations and ceremonies often involved a display of the country's armed forces. Soldiers all around the world wore quite similar camouflaged clothing on the battlefield. However, on the parade ground, military costumes were designed for display, with bright colors and stylish details, which gave clues to the nation's military alliances and other cultural influences. For example, the wide parade cap worn by Russian soldiers influenced the design of military headgear worn in countries such as Kazakhstan, once they regained independence after decades of Soviet occupation. Soldiers' uniforms and medals varied depending on their experience and rank.

Military Leaders

National leaders were often also commanders of the nation's armed forces. Military costume allowed a politician to signal that he was acting in his role as military chief. Some political leaders preferred to remain in civilian clothing, even during a war. Saddam Hussein, dictator of Iraq from 1979 to 2003, generally wore civilian clothing, but dressed all his ministers in army uniforms.

Royalty

Kings, queens, princes, and princesses

The uniform worn by King Bhumibol of Thailand to receive Queen Elizabeth II of England in 1996 displayed his role as head of his country's navy.

sometimes used costumes to indicate their important position as representatives of their nation. Royals were among the few people in public life who could wear extremely formal or traditional clothing. The seriousness of their office, and their ancient family histories, made odd costume details such as feathers in the hat more acceptable in public.

The kings of Swaziland and KwaZulu-Natal in southern Africa had a range of costumes to suit each occasion. Both normally wore a simple item of clothing with just a few symbols of their high office, such as headgear or jewels. At some ceremonies, however, they wore their most impressive and formal costume, symbolizing the full depth of the historical tradition and political stability they represented.

In 1996, King Bhumibol of Thailand celebrated fifty years on the throne. During the festivities, which lasted for several months, he wore many costumes, including a naval officer's white uniform, and royal robes covered with jewels, medals, and other badges of office. The king's royal regalia included a sixteen-pound (7.25-kg) golden crown, a golden sword, scepter, slippers, fan, and whip, all set with precious stones. Some Thai citizens presented the king with the world's largest faceted diamond, renamed the Golden Jubilee, and it was set into the royal scepter.

By the end of the twentieth century, costumes marking royalty out as

Nazi Costume

Costumes played an important part in public life in the 1930s, as supporters of European dictators such as Mussolini and Hitler used military-style uniforms in their political activities. The German Nazi Party organized its own paramilitary force called the SA, or stormtroopers. They dressed in surplus German army uniforms, including brown desert-fighting shirts. The "brownshirts" became a symbol of German pride at Nazi Party rallies and events, at one point exceeding three million members.

unique and wealthy had become less popular. Many royal families—especially in democracies such as Japan and Denmark—preferred to be seen as ordinary people, dressing in plain clothes and expressing their unique place in society by other means, such as charity work.

Dressed in colorful cloth, Zulu and Swazi warriors dance together in South Africa. The sticks they carry are traditional, club-like weapons called knobkerries.

Timeline

1900	The first electric clothes washers appear.
1906	Mariano Fortuny brings out his first "Delphos" gowns.
1909	Mariano Fortuny patents his pleating process.
1910	The first rayon plant opens in the United States.
1911	Paul Poiret launches his "hobble skirt."
1914	Patents for the brassière and the zip fastener.
1920	Coco Chanel introduces yachting trousers for women.
1922	Discovery of Tutankhamun's tomb starts a craze for Egyptian-style textiles.
1928	Adrian creates the "slouch hat" for Greta Garbo.
1930	Sanford L. Cluett patents his method of preshrinking fabric. The invention of Neoprene.
1931	Lastex (elastic) yarn is introduced.
1934	René Lacoste launches his short-sleeved tennis shirt, with a crocodile logo on the chest.
1935	DuPont patents nylon.
1938	*Vogue* publishes its first annual American issue.
1940	Claire McCardell starts her own fashion label.
1941	The invention of polyester, patented as Terylene.
1942	The American navy issues the T-shirt. Clothes rationing begins in the United States.
1946	Launch of the bikini.
1947	Christian Dior launches his Corolle line collection, soon nicknamed the "New Look."
1953	Norman Hartnell designs Queen Elizabeth II's coronation gown.
1956	George de Mestral perfects Velcro. Cristobal Balenciaga creates his "sack dress."
1959	DuPont trademarks Lycra. Spandex is invented.
1963	Weight Watchers is founded, recruiting half a million dieters in its first year.
1964	André Courrèges and Pierre Cardin each launch a "Space Age" collection. Vidal Sassoon creates his "Five-Point Cut" bob.
1965	Yves Saint Laurent creates his "Mondrian" dress. Paco Rabanne makes his first plastic dress.
1966	DuPont patents Kevlar, invented by Stephanie Kwolek.
1969	American clothing store the Gap opens, originally selling only jeans.
1971	US sports' footwear company Nike is founded.
1978	Ralph Lauren launches his "Prairie" collection. Gore-Tex® is patented.
1981	Armani Jeans opens. Polartec fleece is invented.
1983	The first Swatch goes on sale. Karl Lagerfeld becomes design director at Chanel.
1985	Levi 501 jeans are relaunched.
1990	Rifat Ozbek first shows an all-white collection.
1992	Lyocell first made.
1996	Speedo produces its Aquablade swimwear.

Glossary

A-line Narrow at the top and widening at the bottom, like the shape of a letter "A."

army surplus Leftover military clothing supplies that are sold off to civilians.

articulated Made up of different sections, for greater freedom of movement.

balaclava A hood that covers the face and neck, with an opening for the eyes.

bias-cut Describes garments made of cloth that has been cut against the grain, a technique that uses more fabric but allows it to hang better.

boater A man's straw hat with a colored ribbon above the rim.

bolero A short jacket.

brocade A silky fabric with a raised design woven into it.

brogues Shoes that have a pattern of holes punched into the leather.

calico 1. A coarse, colorful printed cotton. 2. A cotton cloth imported from Calcutta, India.

catwalk A narrow stage paraded on by models at a fashion show.

cheesecloth A lightweight, loosely woven cotton cloth, originally used for making cheeses.

chiffon A thin, fine fabric, such as silk or nylon.

choker A close-fitting necklace.

cloche A tight-fitting woman's hat, brimmed or brimless, worn low over the forehead.

corset A close-fitting bodice.

couturier A fashion designer.

cravat A neckerchief worn instead of a tie.

crêpe de chine A finely wrinkled fabric, originally from China.

denim A twilled, dyed cotton used for jeans.

depression A period of reduced economic activity and increased poverty.

derby A man's hat, hard with a round crown and a brim that curves up at the sides. In Britain, the derby is known as a "bowler hat."

dirndl A full skirt, gathered at the waist so as to fall in soft pleats.

epaulettes Military-style shoulder straps on a coat or jacket.

flannel A soft woolen fabric.

flapper A young woman of the twenties, who wore the latest fashions and spent her time dancing and partying.

gabardine (1) Twill-weave fabric with a diagonal rib effect. (2) A trademarked waterproof cotton cloth invented by Thomas Burberry in the 1880s.

gauntlets Long gloves, usually reaching the elbow.

gingham A lightweight fabric, woven from dyed yarns to create a checked pattern.

globalization The process of bringing together different societies from around the world into one global society, due to improved communications.

harem pants Full trousers gathered into a band at the ankle, based on the traditional dress of Turkish women.

haute couture High-quality fashion design, from the French words meaning high and sewing. In haute couture, garments are made to measure.

kohl Black powder, sometimes formed into a pencil, used as eye makeup.

lapels The turned-back part of a jacket's front neckline.

lounge suit A man's matching jacket and pants.

mass production The manufacture of goods in large quantities through the use of standard designs and assembly-line methods.

nautical Describes something having to do with sailors or ships.

nylon A synthetic fabric that is strong and takes dye well.

pedalpushers Calf-length trousers.

peroxide Short for "hydrogen peroxide," the bleach used to dye hair blonde.

pintuck A very narrow, ornamental fold in the fabric.

plaid A twilled woolen fabric with a tartan pattern.

platforms Shoes or boots with extra-thick, built-up heels.

Further Information

rationing Controlling goods that are in short supply, such as foodstuffs or clothes, in time of shortage.

rayon Artificial silk, made from wood pulp or chips.

ready-to-wear Describes fashion garments that are ready made rather than made to measure.

regalia The emblems of royalty.

satin A smooth fabric with one shiny side and one dull—for example, silk or rayon.

scepter A staff or mace carried as a symbol of royalty.

separates Garments designed to be worn interchangeably with others to create different combinations.

shoulder pads Foam pads sewn into the shoulders of jackets or dresses in order to make the wearer appear more broad shouldered.

Soviet Union Also known as the USSR (Union of Soviet Socialist Republics), a country formed from the territories of the Russian Empire in 1917, which lasted until 1991.

suffragette A woman who campaigned for women's right to vote.

synthetic Manmade.

taffeta A shiny, stiff cloth—for example of silk or rayon.

tie-dyed Describes fabric that has been knotted before dyeing, in order to achieve swirling patterns.

trilby A felt hat with a dented crown and flexible brim.

tulle A fine, meshed fabric, originally made of gauze or silk.

tuxedo A dark-colored dinner jacket with silk lapels.

tweed A coarse, woolen fabric, woven into colored patterns.

Adult Reference Sources

Cosgrave, Bronwyn, *The Complete History of Costume and Fashion from Ancient Egypt to the Present Day* (Facts On File, 2000)

Laver, James, *Costume and Fashion* (Thames and Hudson, 1995)

Martin, Richard, *American Ingenuity: Sportswear 1930s–1970s* (Yale University Press, 1998)

O'Hara Callan, Georgina, *Dictionary of Fashion and Fashion Designers* (Thames and Hudson, 1998)

O'Hara, Georgina, *The Encyclopedia of Fashion* (Thames and Hudson, 1996)

Peacock, John, *Chronicle of Western Costume* (Thames and Hudson, 1991)

Peacock, John, *Fashion Accessories: The Complete Twentieth Century Sourcebook* (Thames and Hudson, 2000)

Peacock, John, *Twentieth Century Fashion: The Complete Sourcebook* (Thames and Hudson, 1993)

Young Adult Reference Sources

Baker, Patricia, *Fashions of a Decade: The 1940s* (Facts On File, 1992)

Baker, Patricia, *Fashions of a Decade: The 1950s* (Facts On File, 1991)

Blackman, Cally, *Twentieth Century Fashion: The 20s and 30s* (Heinemann Library, 1999)

Carnegy, Vicky, *Fashions of a Decade: The 1980s* (Facts On File, 1990)

Connikie, Yvonne, *Fashions of a Decade: The 1960s* (Facts On File, 1990)

Costantino, Maria, *Fashions of a Decade: The 1930s* (Facts On File, 1992)

Feldman, Elane, *Fashions of a Decade: The 1990s* (Facts On File, 1992)

Gilmour, Sarah, *Twentieth Century Fashion: The 70s* (Heinemann Library, 1999)

Herald, Jacqueline, *Fashions of a Decade: The 1920s* (Facts On File, 1991)

Herald, Jacqueline, *Fashions of a Decade: The 1970s* (Facts On File, 1992)

Lomas, Clare, *Twentieth Century Fashion: The 80s and 90s* (Heinemann Library, 1999)

Mee, Sue, *Twentieth Century Fashion: 1900–20* (Heinemann Library, 1999)

Powe-Temperley, Kitty, *Twentieth Century Fashion: The 60s* (Heinemann Library, 1999)

Reynolds, Helen, *Twentieth Century Fashion: The 40s and 50s* (Heinemann Library, 1999)

Internet Resources

http://www.vintageblues.com/history_main.htm
A comprehensive history of fashion in the twentieth century.

http://www.fashion-era.com/sitemap.htm
Pages on all aspects of fashion, including social history, sports fashions, underwear, and accessories.

http://www.manchestergalleries.org/html/costume/goc_home.jsp
The website of the Gallery of Costume, Manchester, home to one of Britain's largest fashion collections.

http://www.dressforsuccess.nl/
Includes a useful database of modern fashion designers, as well as a whole section of links related to the history of fashion.

http://www.costumes.org/history/100pages/religious_costume.htm
Links to articles on religious costume, including Jewish, Christian, and Muslim.

http://www.geocities.com/flapper_culture/
A guide to twenties' flapper culture.

http://www.france.diplomatie.fr/label_france/ENGLISH/DOSSIER/MODE/MOD.html
A good basic introduction to some of the big names in twentieth-century French couture.

http://inventors.about.com/library/inventors/blfabric.htm
How some of today's synthetic fabrics were invented.

http://www.fibersource.com/f-tutor/prods.htm
Information on some artificial fibers, not just those used in fashion.

Index